THE

GHOSTLY TALES

OF

BAY CITY,
MICHIGAN

Published by Arcadia Children's Books
A Division of Arcadia Publishing, Inc.
Charleston, SC
www.arcadiapublishing.com

First published 2024
Manufactured in the United States

Designed by Jessica Nevins
Images used courtesy of Shutterstock.com; pp. 6-7 Bernie Parsons/Shutterstock.com;
p. 8 John McCullough/File:USS Edson Intrepid Sea-Air-Space Museum NY 2003.jpg/
Wikimedia Commons/CC BY-SA 2.5; pp. 14-15 Craig Sterken/Shutterstock.com;
pp. 52-53 Roberto GalanShutterstock.com; pp. 92-93 Roberto Galan/Shutterstock.com.

ISBN: 978-1-4671-9755-7
Library of Congress Control Number: 2024930944

Notice: The information in this book is true and complete to the best of our
knowledge. It is offered without guarantee on the part of the author or Arcadia
Publishing. The author and Arcadia Publishing disclaim all liability in connection with
the use of this book.

Spooky America

THE
GHOSTLY TALES
OF
BAY CITY, MICHIGAN

946

ANNA LARDINOIS

Adapted from Haunted Bay City, Michigan by Nicole Beauchamp

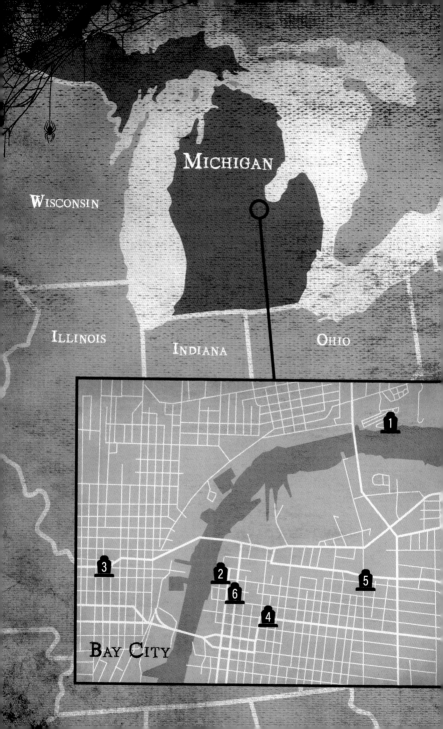

TABLE OF CONTENTS & MAP KEY

Welcome to Spooky Bay City!

At first glance, Bay City, Michigan, might not seem like the spookiest place on Earth. With its beautiful sandy beaches, welcoming waterfront, colorful candy shops, and bustling restaurants, this charming town on Lake Huron's Saginaw Bay couldn't *possibly* be a supernatural hot spot . . . could it?

Well, if you've ever heard someone say there are no ghosts in Bay City, you can assure them

they are dead wrong. Because—SURPRISE!—
Bay City is full of spirits!

In this book, you'll meet Paul, the spirit
of a man who lived and died on the historic
USS *Edson* (now the home of the celebrated
Saginaw Valley Naval Ship Museum). You'll
also get to know Charlie, one of the many
apparitions that appear in the Scottish Rite
Masonic Center. You'll encounter more than
one ghost that does not respect the privacy of
the living when they are using the bathroom.
And that's just for starters!

If you are brave enough to turn the pages,
you will also discover a haunted store filled
with treasures from the past. Too bad those
treasures are haunted! You'll definitely want
to read that story before your family decides to
bring any antiques into your house!

If you make it all the way to the end of this

book, you will never, ever think there are no ghosts in Bay City! You will meet plenty of them! But, you might just wonder which ghosts are still out there, yet to be discovered.

So, gather your courage and get ready to discover the *spooktacular* side of Bay City. The ghosts are waiting for you in all their creepy glory. All you have to do is turn the page.

Are you brave enough?

Bay City, Michigan

The Eerie USS Edson

The most haunted place in Bay City is one of the city's top tourist attractions. Each year, thousands of people visit the Saginaw Valley Naval Ship Museum to tour the USS *Edson*. Known as Bay City's Gray Ghost, the naval destroyer was built in 1959 and served the U.S. Navy all over the world before it was decommissioned in 1988. The ship has been in Bay City since 2012.

Listed as a National Historic Landmark, this massive ship is longer than a football field and weighs a whopping 2,800 tons. And one more thing—it's haunted!

Bay City resident Bill Randall served in the Navy for six years, where he worked aboard a naval destroyer. He began volunteering at the Saginaw Valley Naval Ship Museum as a tour guide in 2013. He remembers a sweltering August many summers ago when he participated in a ghost-hunting event aboard the *Edson*.

Bill led the group of seven paranormal investigators to the lowest level of the ship they could access. This section of the ship had no electricity, so the only light in the inky darkness below deck came from the handheld flashlights a few of the ghosthunters carried. The group climbed down ladders and stairwells until they reached the room farthest from the surface of the water: the boatswain's locker.

A boatswain is the worker on a boat who maintains the outside of the boat. A boatswain paints the boat and is responsible for the deck and other topside duties. Even though it is called a locker, the boatswain's locker is really just a small closet where they store the equipment needed to do their job.

The group huddled in the small dark room far below the water's surface. The August air was hot and dripping with humidity. No breeze could reach the group, and sweat beaded on their foreheads and trickled down their faces.

Suddenly, one of the investigators—who was from England—noticed a change in the room. A chill crept into the small space. She wondered if the cold air she felt was the presence of an unseen spirit.

Quickly, another investigator in the group turned on a spirit box the team had brought on board. A spirit box is a device used by paranormal researchers to communicate with spirits. The boxes work by quickly scanning AM and FM radio signals. Some people believe that spirits can use those frequencies to speak or share a message with the living. Once the spirit box was switched on, the room grew even colder. Soon, the investigator from England was shivering.

"Is anyone here with us?" she asked through chattering teeth.

A faint voice came from the spirit box. "Yes," the voice murmured softly.

"Thanks for your response," the investigator said, "but could you please tell us your name?"

The spirit box again crackled to life. The voice that came through was much stronger this time. "My name is Paul," said the voice, which sounded like that of an adult man.

"Paul, when did you pass away?" asked the investigator.

The voice grew faint again. The investigators could not understand what the spirit said, but it seemed as if the number ended in a "nine."

At the very moment the spirit box whispered out the number nine, one of the investigators felt an unseen arm wrap around her waist. The young woman was on the second level of the boatswain's locker. In the dark, she had moved too close to an opening in the floor. Before she realized she was in danger, she was pulled back

USS *Edson*

so she did not fall. The arm that saved her did not belong to anyone in the group of ghost hunters. It was the very spirit the group was communicating with!

When the woman later spoke about the event, she said she wasn't scared when the spirit grabbed her. Instead, she felt safe and protected.

The next day, Bill was talking to the other volunteers about what had happened below deck the night before. The group of volunteers jumped on their computers and began to investigate men named Paul connected with the history of the USS *Edson*. It didn't take the volunteers long to discover Paul Spampanato.

At one time, Paul lived aboard the ship and served both as the *Edson*'s caretaker and tour guide. Once the volunteers dug a little further, they found out that many people have had paranormal experiences with Paul's spirit.

According to their research, Paul is most often seen wearing a khaki-colored shirt and pants. He walks throughout the ship as if he is still in charge of maintaining it.

One day, museum president Michael Kegley and volunteer Jack Pennell were watching the surveillance camera aboard the ship when they saw something that stunned them both. They spotted a man in a khaki outfit walking on the ship's main deck. His back was to the camera, and as he walked away, his body *disappeared*. There was not a trace of him! When the men talked about the unbelievable sight they had just witnessed, they agreed the man captured on camera bore a striking resemblance to the photo they'd seen of Paul Spampanato.

Visitors to the *Edson* have snapped many photos of Paul over the years. There are photos of the khaki-clad man on the decks and in places on the ship closed to the public.

Thanks to the many sightings of Paul, Bill Randall is now a firm believer in the afterlife. Bill thinks the spirit that remains aboard is a prankster. Visitors report being tapped on the shoulder or having their hair tugged by an unseen hand while touring the ship. Bill believes all of these instances are just Paul having a little fun in the afterlife.

Tim Shaw, a well-known lecturer and medium (a medium is a person who can make contact and communicate with spirits), had his own experience with a spirit believed to be Paul while attending a paranormal event on the *Edson*. After several hours of investigation on the ship, the attendees decided to take a break. As Tim rested in a room below deck, he felt a strong and sudden sensation that someone was watching him.

Tim slowly turned around and saw the shadowy figure of a man's body. Instead of a face, the form had a "featureless white head that resembled an over-pixelated digital image." Tim was stunned. "It smoothly began to turn away from us as if it were moving on ball bearings," he said. Tim jumped up and ran after the figure. He dashed through hallways and different rooms, following the being, but it slipped away before Tim could catch up to it.

Later, investigators spoke with Bill Randall about Tim's eerie experience, and Bill told the investigators about Paul. They also found out that Paul died in the room where Tim encountered the otherworldly being!

Thinking back on the event, Tim says, "This was one of the few peak personal experiences that I will remember for a very long time."

Many paranormal investigators believe that Paul is just one of the many spirits that still linger on the *Edson*. Experts think there may be as many as eight spirits on the ship, including a ghostly dog!

The USS *Edson* sits in the Saginaw River waiting for people to explore its history. I'm sure Paul would be happy to show you around if you climb aboard! That is, if you dare!

The Alarming
Antique Center

Have you ever been to the Bay City Antique Center on North Water Street? The building is in the middle of what Bay City residents used to call "Hell's Half Mile." The area earned that nickname in the years between 1865-1900, because it was the rowdiest and most dangerous part of town.

Today, the neighborhood is much tamer, but be on your guard if you pay a visit to the

Bay City Antique Center. Instead of avoiding fistfights and gambling dens, you'll need to avoid the ghostly beings that have made this building their home.

It seems as if the building has been haunted for as long as anyone in Bay City can remember. The building was originally used as office and retail space, but in 1868, it became the Campbell House Hotel. The hotel changed owners, and in 1920, it was converted into two separate businesses. In 1931, a furniture store called C. E. Rosenbury and Sons took over the entire space, and it operated in the building for fifty-four years before the current owners, Bill and Elaine Fournier, bought it and turned

it into a large antique mall. The couple soon discovered the building came with ghosts.

"Rosenbury's employees told us that they would be all closed down for the night, ready to leave and would hear footsteps upstairs," Elaine said. "When they went to locate what they presumed was an errant shopper, there would be no one there."

It didn't take long for Elaine and Bill to have a few strange stories of their own. "There were offices in the basement of the building and several times when employees had arrived at work in the morning, papers would be all over the place, despite things being in good order the night before," said Elaine.

Elaine's teenaged children had some eerie experiences in the building that terrified them. "Often, we would work very late into the evening," Elaine recalled. "There was an intercom system throughout the store which was left up by the previous owners. The kids would turn on the intercom that monitored the second floor and listen. They reported hearing all sorts of noises."

Whatever the boys heard on the intercom upset them so much that one of her sons refused to step foot on the second floor without his trusty German shepherd at his side. Elaine tried to discover what had happened to make her son so frightened. The boy told her that he'd felt something physically pass through his body while on the second floor. It was an experience he never wanted to have again!

It seems as if the second floor is just as scary for customers as it is for those who work in the old building. Bay City resident Ashley Harris had an experience on that seemingly haunted floor she will never forget.

One rainy afternoon, Ashley stopped at the antique mall to look for additions to her vinyl record collection. The store was nearly empty. The only people inside were Ashley and two store employees. She was excited to have the whole store to herself. She looked forward to taking her time browsing through boxes without having to worry about being in anyone's way.

As the raindrops drummed on the windows, Ashley moved through the first floor of the antique center. She climbed the stairs to the second floor and quickly found an entire box filled with vinyl records.

Ashley eagerly flipped through the box of records when a strange sensation came over her. "I remember experiencing this intense feeling that I was being watched. My hair was standing on end," Ashley said.

She looked up from the box of records and scanned the room. But she was all alone. At least, that is what she thought.

Ashley shrugged off the eerie feeling and returned her attention to the box of records. In moments, she heard the distinct *click-click-click* of a pair of high-heeled shoes walking across the wooden floor. She looked up and tried to catch of glimpse of the other person on the second floor, but she did not see anyone.

"It sounded like someone was getting closer and closer to me," Ashley recalled. "I felt very confused. I did not recall seeing anyone up on that floor, and I couldn't pinpoint where the sound was coming from."

Ashley walked away from the box of records and moved toward the center of the room, determined to catch a glimpse of the person who had joined her on the second floor. She looked around the room but still could not see anyone.

Suddenly, she heard a faint sound. Just a whisper. She turned her head to see where the sound had come from and froze.

It was a woman. At least, she had been when she was alive. Now, she was undeniably a ghost. Ashley stared at the apparition. The ghostly figure was wearing a lacy purple dress in a style that had been popular in the Victorian era. She noticed the spirit's tall, black lace-up boots and her long brown hair twisted into an updo on her ghostly head!

"Her eyes were black, and her face was ashen. It was like she was staring into my soul, her eyes almost glowing from beyond the darkness of her eye sockets and her bruised lips curling into an unsettling grin," Ashley said.

Ashley trembled in fright. She was too scared to move. Her heart was pounding as the spirit took a step closer to her. The ghost raised its index finger toward Ashley. Then, she curled her finger into a gesture meant to get Ashley to step closer to the spirit.

Before Ashley could do anything—run, scream, call for help—the ghostly woman vanished into thin air. "I dropped the records I was holding. I could not breathe. It was like all the air had left my lungs," she recalled.

Ashley ran down the steps and out of the store. She wanted to put as much distance as possible between her and the second floor specter. She ran so quickly, she did not even respond to the employees who wished her a good day as she dashed out the door.

In the days that followed this otherworldly encounter, Ashley began to share her story. She was surprised when some people were skeptical, but she knew the truth. "I know what I saw," Ashely said. "People can think whatever they want. I know for certain that what I saw was an actual ghost. I haven't slept with the lights off since," she said.

Ashley isn't the only customer to have an otherworldly encounter inside the antique mall. Though he passed away in 2023, Bay City resident and paranormal enthusiast Harold Beauchamp Jr. also had a spinetingling experience while shopping in the building.

Harold served the country in the U.S. Marine Corps, and loved to collect rare military memorabilia. One morning, he and his wife Ellen visited the store to see if they could find any interesting pieces to add to his collection.

While strolling through the store, Harold found an olive-colored cap with a black visor. Attached to the hat was a U.S. Marine Corps pin. It was a Marine's visor cap from World War II. Harold couldn't believe his good luck! "I'm a hat collector, so it was really neat to find something like this," he'd explained at the time. "Especially in such great condition!" He grabbed the hat from the shelf and held on to it. It would be a great addition to his collection.

Harold carried the hat as he continued to look through the aisles for more treasures. As

he strolled the store, he suddenly heard the voice of a woman whisper into his left ear. The voice said, "Hey, what are you doing with that hat?"

"Ellen, you won't believe what year this is from," Harold replied. He turned to show his wife the hat, but she wasn't there. No one was. He was completely alone. Harold was confused as he stood in the empty aisle. Ellen had just been there a moment ago when she'd whispered in his ear. Hadn't she?

The voice whispered again. This time, it was right behind him. "I'm right here," the voice hissed. Harold looked up and saw Ellen walking toward him from across the room. His heart beat faster. If Ellen was walking toward him, who had whispered to him from behind?

"Elly, was that you just talking to me?" Harold asked his wife.

Now it was Ellen's turn to be confused. "No," she replied. "I was looking at purses. I was not anywhere near you. You know that."

Harold was shaken. He wasn't sure what had just happened, but he suspected it had something to do with the hat he'd discovered. He couldn't prove it, but he wondered if maybe there was a spirit connected to that hat. Harold carefully returned the hat to the shelf where he'd found it. He decided it was best to leave the hat—and whatever supernatural force was connected to it—alone. Harold left the store without the hat, but with a strange and spooky tale to tell. Though he is sadly no longer collecting hats, Harold sure did love them while he was living.

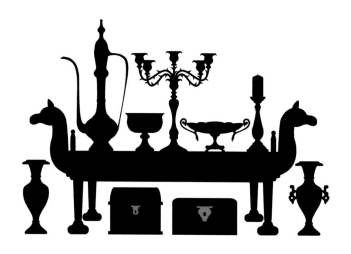

What do you think? Have the spirits and souls at the Bay City Antique Center been there throughout the building's long history? Or might these ghosts have come to reside here because of their attachment to the antiques the Fourniers buy and sell?

If it's possible that spirits can "live" inside old objects, that means you must be *very* careful about what you bring into your home. The old adage "finders keepers, losers weepers," could easily turn into "finders weepers!"

Don't say you haven't been warned.

The Spooky Sage Library

Some places just *look* haunted—do you know what I mean? In my opinion, one of those places is the Sage Public Library. I am not sure what it is about the red brick library built in 1884 by Henry Sage, but every time I see it, I get the willies!

They say you can't judge a book by its cover, but in the case of the Sage Public Library, it seems like you can. Because not only does this place look haunted, but it actually *is* haunted!

Just about everyone in Bay City knows that something otherworldly resides in the library. Some say the strange and spooky nighttime activity here is connected to the way Henry Sage got the money to pay for his extraordinary library. There are rumors that the wealthy lumber baron stole money from a bank account that belonged to his employees to construct the building.

Understandably, the theft made some of Sage's employees mad. Mad enough to rise from the grave and haunt the building that was built using *their* hard-earned money! No one knows for sure if it is Sage's former employees who haunt the building—but there's no doubt that something or someone sure does!

The spirits make their presence known at night, after all the library's visitors have gone home. The library staff have heard the sounds of disembodied footsteps around the building while they lock up the library for the evening. The heavy thud of what sounds like work boots can be heard echoing through the empty staircases as the staff completes their duties for the day.

One staff member remembers closing for the night when she had a terrifying experience. "I had just finished locking the front doors and was doing one last round in the building to make sure everything was in order," she said. "That's when I heard what sounded like

heavy boots stomping behind me. I checked everything out and I didn't see anyone." With fear in her eyes, she continued, "I was creeped out but made it my goal to finish my work quickly so I could get out of there as soon as possible. When I descended the stairwell and got to the landing, I heard the thudding of the boots coming down the stairs after me. All I could do was freeze in terror and gaze upward at the upper levels, praying I wouldn't come face-to-face with whoever was making all that noise."

Fortunately, that library worker never encountered the spirit that followed her through the empty building. But the haunting of the Sage Library involves more than just ghostly footsteps.

Once everyone leaves for the night, it seems the spirits in the library really *come alive*. In the morning, the staff returns to find books pulled from their shelves and arranged in strange patterns. Sometimes the books are placed in tidy piles. Other times, the books appear to have been tossed around by unseen hands. It is not uncommon for the first employee to open the door in the morning to find books scattered across the library floor.

Not all the spirits lingering in the library are unseen, however. For more than one hundred years, people have reported seeing the apparition of a little girl on the third floor.

The young girl wears a long white dress. When people catch a glimpse of the girl's ghostly face, they see that her face is scarred. It looks as if she may have had smallpox or another disease that leaves the skin permanently damaged.

Some believe they know the identity of the ghostly girl. A woman named Miss Ahern wrote to the library on June 18, 1901, to share the story of a small child, known only as Miss Burns, who died after catching smallpox from a library book. Could the otherworldly girl in the white dress be the very same child?

The reports of strange happenings in the library attracted paranormal investigators to the building. In 2013, the Tri-City Ghost Hunters Society conducted an investigation of the Sage Library. This was not the first time the living had tried to connect with the building's otherworldly spirits. Several mediums had also explored the library in the past. A few of them mentioned connecting with a man who seemed rather concerned with the carpeting in the building. In fact, he'd chosen to remain in the library to ensure that his hard work was being maintained!

The Tri-City Ghost Hunters Society had no idea what spirits they might encounter, but they hoped to connect with the young girl in the white dress who generations of library staff and patrons had seen.

The investigators climbed the stairs to the third floor, one of them carrying a spirit box in her arms. The investigators stood under the entrance to the attic, accessed by a drop-down stairway in the ceiling. A member of the team grabbed the rope and pulled it down. Then the brave ghost hunters climbed into the attic.

Once inside the dark attic, the investigators turned on their spirit box. The spirit box immediately began making sounds. The investigators listened carefully and heard a voice! But they did not connect with the child.

The team asked the spirit its name. They were surprised when they heard the voice of an adult man say, "Jacob." They were so surprised, they tried again, thinking something might be wrong with the spirit box. The investigator asked again, "Could you please tell us your name?" expecting a child to respond. Instead, the team heard the male voice say, "I just did." The investigators knew there was nothing wrong with the spirit box. They were communicating with a spirit who called himself Jacob.

After meeting Jacob, the investigators wanted to learn more about him. With the help of librarian Kirsten Grantham-Wellnitz, the team discovered who Jacob might have been when he was among the living.

Back in 1904, a man named Jacob Beck did work at the Sage Library. The man was hired to lay and clean the carpeting. Is Jacob Beck the ghost the investigators encountered? It seems likely. Not only is Jacob Beck the *only* Jacob that appears in the library's records, but he seems to be the same man that mediums have communicated with in the past. Strange and spooky, indeed!

So, why don't you take a look around the Sage Public Library? It is one of the few haunted

buildings you can visit in Bay City when it is open. Or better yet, why don't you read this book INSIDE the Sage Public Library? Do you think that will increase your chances of having

a spinetingling paranormal encounter there? Maybe—just maybe—one of the building's well-known ghosts will stop by and say hello.

A Gentlemanly Ghost

Before we take a look at why people believe the Bay City Scottish Rite Masonic Center on Center Avenue is haunted, let's find out what a Scottish Rite Masonic Center is. The easiest way to do that is to break down the words.

The key word in the building's name is *Masonic*. Masonic means having to do with the Freemasons. The Freemasons is an organization that only men can join. It is said to be the largest and oldest men's group in the world. No one knows for sure, but many people believe the name of the group came from guilds created by stonemasons in the Middle Ages. (A guild is an association of merchants or craftsmen.) The original stonemasons built castles and cathedrals.

Some people think of the Freemasons as a social club that does charitable activities. Others think of it as a secret society full of mysteries.

Now let's find out what Scottish Rite means. This is essentially a type of Freemasonry practiced by members who have reached a high level in the organization. So, all together, Scottish Rite Masonic Center just means a club house for a certain type of Freemason.

Okay, now that we have that all squared

away, let's take a closer look at this haunted building.

Built in 1925, the center served many Masons over the years.

Despite its name, the building is no longer connected to the Freemasons. Today, many people get married inside the grand tan brick building. For some reason, it is often brides who have supernatural experiences in this super-spooky building.

The building's former barbershop has been converted into a place for brides to primp before their wedding ceremony. The women waiting in this room are usually very happy. They are eager to exchange vows with their soon-to-be spouse.

One bride who had her wedding day inside the Masonic Center was no exception. She recalled standing in the bridal room as

Bay City Scottish Rite Masonic Center

she anxiously awaited her cue to make her entrance. As she stood in the doorway in her white gown, she noticed a man in the tunnel just outside the room.

He was an older man, wearing a suit and eyeglasses. The tunnel was dark. The bride peered at the man, but she didn't recognize him. She thought perhaps he worked there and was about to tell her something had gone wrong with the wedding plans. A look of concern came over her face as she asked the man if everything was okay.

The man gave her a dazzling smile. "Oh, darling, you look positively beautiful," he said.

The bride smiled. His kind words made her

heart swell. She opened her mouth to thank him when, without warning, he suddenly disappeared! She blinked. She could not believe her eyes. The man had been there a moment ago. Now he was nowhere to be seen. Where could he possibly have gone?

The stunned bride would later discover she had encountered the apparition of Charles E. Sharp. She was just one of the many brides visited by this ghostly gentleman on their wedding day.

When he was among the living, Charles was a devoted Mason. He reached one of the highest levels of Freemasonry and served as the lodge's secretary for thirty-six years. When he died in 1967, it seems his spirit chose to remain inside the building that had been so meaningful to him in life.

It is not just brides who see the ghostly

image of Charles. According to Chris, the current lodge secretary, he has seen Charles as well. The strange thing is, Chris has only seen the lower half of Charles's form. While brides see the ghost's full body and face, that has never happened for Chris. "Every time I've witnessed him," Chris explained, "it was always just the lower half of his body, with a torso or a leg manifesting first."

Chris might not have seen Charles's face, but the things he has seen in the building will raise the hair on the back of your neck! He has seen things so strange that he is convinced the auditorium is a portal of paranormal activity.

Chris has reported seeing orbs in the auditorium many times. Orbs are glowing balls of light that move through the air on their own. Many people who believe in ghosts think that orbs are actually the spirits of the dead moving in the earthly realm. Orbs can appear in just about any size or color. Sometimes, orbs cannot be seen with the naked eye but will appear in photos and video.

Chris recalls walking into the auditorium and seeing a glowing light out of the corner of his eye. When he turned his head toward the light, he could not believe his eyes. He saw orbs of light bigger than softballs whizzing around the room!

At first, Chris thought there might be something medically wrong with his eyes. But he quickly ruled that out. His eyes were fine.

But what he was seeing sure wasn't! "Based on what I've seen," he said, "I do believe these experiences I've had to be paranormal."

After his experiences with Charles and the orbs, Chris will no longer walk around the building in the dark. "The experiences here have genuinely spooked me," he said.

Chris is not the only one in his family to have possibly had an otherworldly encounter in the building. Each time Chris's three-year-old daughter would visit him at work, she would smile, wave, and say hello as she passed a small doorway that led to the pipe organ. Chris never saw anything outside the door, but his daughter would greet the seemingly empty part of the room every visit. What do you think she could see that the adults around her could not?

Not just the event venue is thought to be

haunted. The upper floors of the building have also had their share of strange occurrences. The Great Lakes Bay Region Children's Dyslexia Center is located on the fifth floor of the building. The center's employees have also encountered Charles.

On her first day as the center's director, the employees warned Nancy Willams that her new workplace was haunted. "If you're here alone late at night and you hear something, just say hello to Charlie and everything will be just fine," Nancy recalls them telling her.

Instead of running out the door in fear, Nancy got to work. And, before long, she started experiencing unexplained events. More than once, when Nancy was alone in the building at night, she heard the unmistakable sound of furniture being moved in the dining room on the floor below. When sounds of chairs being dragged across the floor and tables being rearranged came from the empty dining room, she remembered her colleagues' advice. She always called out a greeting to Charlie into the dark and empty dining room, hoping the spirit activity would cease.

After she had been working in the building for a while, brave Nancy decided she would use the sixth floor to store some items from the center. She liked the attic rooms. They were tucked away from the rest of the building and could only be accessed by a single flight of stairs on the fifth floor.

Late one night, Nancy was working alone in a room near the only entry to the attic.

Suddenly, Nancy heard movement on the sixth floor. She listened to the sound of boxes being moved on the floor above her and felt a chill dart up her spine. She was working right in front of the staircase that led to the sixth floor. There was no other way to reach the attic, and she was certain no one could have entered the staircase without her noticing.

So then . . . *who* was moving the boxes?

Nancy realized that the sounds coming from the attic must be otherworldly. There was no other explanation. The only way to get to the attic was to walk past her and she had not seen anyone all night. And it couldn't have been mice or other attic pests. The storage boxes were so heavy that even an army of mice could not have moved them.

If it wasn't a person and it wasn't and animal, what else could it be but a ghost?

Long ago, some people had used the old attic as a secret place to play poker. Perhaps the spirits that still linger in the building weren't happy with Nancy using their one-time hideaway as a place to store her boxes?

If you believe the stories, not only is the Scottish Rite Masonic Center haunted, but so is the Historic Masonic Temple right next door. The temple was built in 1893. It was then destroyed by a fire in 1903 and eventually rebuilt in 1905. Nick Suchyta, the former director of Bay City's nonprofit Masonic temple preservation group, stated, "I was a skeptic until I started working here."

Working the late-night shift in the temple turned Nick into a believer. "Doors unlock that I *definitely* know I locked. I will go set something down for a second, come back and it is wide open. It's left me and the other volunteers totally puzzled," he said.

Nick listened to music on his night shifts. He didn't do this to make the time pass more quickly. He did it because he NEEDED to! "I have to play it to drown out the voices," confessed Nick. "I hear male and female voices conversing all night long."

Is Charlie one of the otherworldly chatterboxes that Nick heard? It's possible! Gary Conklin, a member who used to clean the temple, has seen Charlie's ghostly figure in the building.

One night when Gary was cleaning up, he opened the door to the game room. What he saw on the other side of the door stopped him in his tracks.

Inside the room was a lively scene from the 1930s! He was astonished as he watched the roomful of men dressed in suits from a bygone era. He could hear the men talking and laughing as they smoked their cigars. They carried on as if Gary was not there at all.

Stunned, Gary blinked his eyes. In an instant, the men and their party were gone. He was staring into a dark and empty room.

Gary ran to find Chris. He had to tell someone about the extraordinary thing he just witnessed.

He expected that no one would believe such an incredible tale. He was wrong. Chris had already experienced so much ghostly activity in the building he had no trouble believing every word Gary said about his hair-raising vision.

However, it appears more than ghostly Masons roam these buildings. There have been many reports of the apparition of a young woman showing herself to the living.

The first time paranormal investigator Johna Shorey saw the ghostly girl in the lodge, she thought it was someone wearing a creepy costume. Johna was at the temple as part of a haunted attraction fundraiser. It made sense to her that a volunteer would hide in a dark shadow in the corner of the room, waiting to scare visitors at the event.

The nearly hidden figure seemed to be

about twelve years old, and her appearance was truly frightening. Her head hung so low that her long, black hair completely covered her face, and her arms dangled limply by her sides. When Johna took a second look at the girl, she realized in shock that she was looking at a ghost!

The Friends of the Historic Masonic Temple's treasurer, Kelley Kent, has also encountered an apparition of a young girl in the building. The ghost that Johna saw was frightening, but the one that Kelley saw was more frightened than frightening!

Kelley was also working at a haunted attraction fundraiser when she encountered a ghostly girl. Kelley was climbing the stairs to the billiards room when she saw a little girl peeking out from the staircase banister. The girl looked to be somewhere between eight and twelve years old. She had short, blond hair cut in a bob and was wearing a white blouse, plaid skirt, long stockings, and Mary Jane-style shoes. The young girl pressed herself against the wall, as if trying to get away from Kelley.

The child stared back at Kelley with wide eyes. Just as Kelley was about to speak to the girl, she vanished!

The spirits of these young girls are just two of the many ghosts that have been spotted in the building and around the property. Others report seeing the ghostly form of a very young girl with brown hair, a middled-aged man wearing a top hat and smoking a cigar, and a beautiful young woman with flowing golden hair wearing an elegant violet dress.

If you are wondering why there is so much paranormal activity in the Scottish Rite and Historic Masonic Temple, it might be because both buildings were constructed on top of an old cemetery. It is said that the bodies originally laid to rest on the land were exhumed—or dug up—and reburied at the Oak Ridge Cemetery. Could the gravediggers have missed a corpse or two when clearing the land? If so, it may explain the *many* otherworldly happenings in these Bay City landmarks.

If all this isn't enough to scare you away from Center Avenue, I don't know what else

could! Just a reminder, if you do visit the Scottish Rite Masonic Center or the Historic Masonic Temple, don't forget to say hello to Charlie. If you don't, you just might have your *own* hair-raising encounter with the spirits!

CHAPTER 5

Spirits in the Sweets Shop

Is there anything better than a candy shop? Visitors to the Tummy Ache Candy Store on North Johnson Street always take a deep breath when they walk into the shop, inhaling the heavenly aromas that fill the air. Jars filled with every kind of sugary sweet imaginable line the shelves, and the homemade ice cream treats are hard to resist.

The shop offers so much more than just sweet treats. It also has a wonderful selection of spirits that have made the shop their home.

The building was built back in 1920, and over the years, it was home to several different businesses. Then, in 2000, Starr and Michael Henning bought the building. The creative business owners wanted to do everything they could to make the store a fun place for people to visit. They added decorations inspired by magical stories, like *Charlie and the Chocolate Factory* and *Alice in Wonderland*.

One day, while the Hennings were working to get the shop ready for business, something strange happened. Michael was in the back of the building using a jackhammer to break up cement. He couldn't hear a thing over the jackhammer's racket.

At the same time, Starr was working in the front. She was organizing some wood the couple would use for an upcoming project in the candy store. Starr was so focused on her work that she forgot a log was on the ground behind her.

While holding a large piece of wood with very sharp edges, Starr stepped backward and stumbled on the log. She fell to the ground, and the wood she had been working with fell on top of her. She was laying under a pile of wood when she called out to Michael.

"Please, help me!" she screamed at the top

of her lungs. But Michael had no idea Starr was in trouble. Her cries for help could not be heard over the pounding of the jackhammer.

As Starr lay under the fallen lumber, she noticed she wasn't in as much pain as she should have been. She carefully wiggled her fingers and toes.

As she started to pull the pieces of wood off her body, she looked at her arms and saw they were fine. No bloody wounds or red welts. The same thing happened when she uncovered her

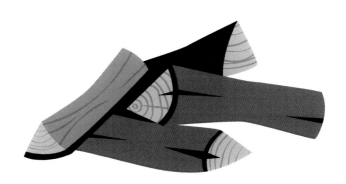

legs. Unbelievably, not only didn't she have any broken bones, there wasn't a single scratch on her! To Starr, it seemed impossible that she had not been seriously injured in the accident. Well, *almost* impossible.

Starr sensed that an otherworldly being had protected her from serious injury.

Ever since Starr was a little girl, she believed she had some sort of spiritual ability. As she sat on the ground surrounded by the fallen lumber, she suddenly felt the presence of an unseen man in the room. She sensed he was there to protect her. She also believed that he knew she had spiritual abilities. Starr relaxed, somehow knowing the man was there to help her.

Little did she know, Starr would not be the *only* one in the Henning family to have an encounter with the unseen man.

Michael and Starr have a son named Sky. He grew up in the shop and helped his parents with various jobs. When he wasn't helping, he would play in the back of the shop. One day while playing, Sky suddenly heard a voice calling him: "Sky! Come here, Sky!"

The boy stopped what he was doing and immediately ran to where his mother was working.

"Mom, was that you calling for me? Do you need my help?" Sky asked.

"No, Honey, I wasn't calling for you," she answered.

That was strange. Sky was certain he'd heard a voice calling for him from the candy shop. His mom didn't have an explanation for what had happened, and eventually, the two just forgot about it.

That is, until the next time it happened.

And the time after that. And the time after *that*. Soon, a voice starting calling for Sky ALL the time!

Every time he heard the voice call his name, he'd run to find his parents only to discover that neither his mom nor his dad was looking for him. Eventually, the family learned that the otherworldly being lingering in the building was a bit of a prankster.

It seems that the spirit calling Sky also liked to pester people who used the restroom at the Tummy Ache Candy Store.

Starr walked into the restroom one day. As she closed the door, she felt an unseen hand touch her—on her bottom! Starr was not amused by the prank, and she let the spirit know it. It was clear the ghost understood because he never did it again.

But that doesn't mean the spirit stopped

playing games in the restroom. A shop employee was using the restroom when the door suddenly flew open—*while* the shop was crowded with customers! It may have amused the ghost, but the exposed employee didn't think the prank was very funny.

The prankster ghost makes its presence known in other, less embarrassing ways as well.

The spirit likes to mess with the music being played in the shop. On a regular basis, the entity will adjust the volume of the stereo, sometimes turning the music up as loud as it can go. Other times, the spirit will simply turn the stereo off, leaving the candy shop in stunned silence.

It isn't just the employees who have had otherworldly encounters in Tummy Ache Candy Store. A regular customer had an unusual experience in the store , too.

During the holidays, the customer was shopping in the store with her four-year-old daughter. The mother and daughter were having fun looking at all the special holiday candy. The mother had been carrying two twenty-dollar bills in her hand as they shopped.

As they were deciding what treats to buy, the mom suddenly realized the money in her hand was gone. She began to retrace her steps, carefully looking for the cash that had seemingly disappeared.

She searched everywhere but could not find the lost money. Just as she was about to tell her daughter they couldn't buy any candy that day, she heard a man's voice whisper loudly in her ear.

"Check the Jolly Ranchers," the voice said. The woman turned to see who had spoken to her, but no one was there.

Puzzled, she walked to a shelf full of jars of different hard candies. When she located the jar full of Jolly Ranchers, she lifted the glass

lid. Inside, she saw the two twenty-dollar bills! The woman was stunned. She was *positive* she had not opened any of the jars while she had been shopping. And, even if she had, she knew she would never put her money in a candy jar.

Without an earthly explanation, the woman concluded the store's ghost must have placed the money in the jar to keep it safe until she found it.

After hearing the many tales of strange happenings in the candy store, two paranormal investigators decided to pay a visit in 2017. Ray and Alan are experienced ghost hunters who brought equipment with them to detect the presence of paranormal activity.

They brought a spirit box to scan the radio waves in search of spirits, and a Mel Meter, a device that measures both the room temperature and the area's electromagnetic field. Many ghost hunters believe the presence of a spirit will cause cold spots and other unexplained drops in temperature. They also believe that the unseen spirit can be detected by a sudden increase in the electromagnetic field. A Mel Meter allows investigators to measure both of these things at the same time.

Starr joined the ghost hunters. Before the investigation began, they shut off the building's electricity so it wouldn't interfere with any of the special equipment the ghost hunters were using.

During the investigation, Starr began to talk to the man she thought had protected her when she fell. As soon as she began to speak to the spirit, the Mel Meter showed a spike in the electromagnetic field! Was the ghostly man in the room with them? It sure seemed like it!

But that was not the only paranormal energy the ghost hunters detected. When the investigators began to use the spirit box, they got some startling results!

Investigators heard the name "Tessa" repeated over and over again while listening to the box. Who was Tessa? What about the man who had helped Starr and often pranked Sky?

After hearing the name Tessa, Starr called out into the seemingly empty room. "Is Tessa here now?" she asked.

The investigators were stunned when Starr received an answer!

"Don't worry, Alan," replied a voice through the spirit box. "Find Tessa."

The three couldn't believe it—the spirit had called one of the investigators by name!

Eager to continue the connection with this otherworldly being, Starr asked the unseen spirit named Tessa to sit next to her.

Instantly, all the paranormal activity meters they'd set up around the building began to register activity! You might think Starr was afraid, but she was excited! She continued talking to the spirits in the room. The more she spoke to them, the stronger she felt their presence. The connection between Starr and the unseen being strengthened. Soon, Starr heard her own name come from the spirit box! The spirits were trying to communicate with her!

The investigation never revealed who Tessa was, or why her spirit remains in the candy shop, but Starr doesn't mind. She is happy to have met this peaceful spirit that has made the Tummy Ache Candy Store its home.

Oftentimes, ghosts can be scary, but the ones that linger in the candy shop seem to be quite cheerful! Maybe they like being around all the ice cream, chocolates, and other goodies so much, they forget to be frightening? It is hard to say, but the people who visit all seem to think the building is filled with positive energy.

It seems like the perfect place to begin a search for spirits. Even if you don't experience something otherworldly, you'll still have the chance to get some very tasty treats!

But, maybe you should skip using the bathroom in the shop. Just in case. You never know when the door might fly open again and leave you, uh—exposed!

The Spine-Tingling State Theatre

Have you ever seen a show at the State Theatre? That old theater on Washington Avenue has quite a history. It was built in 1908. Back then, it was called the Bijou, and it had live performances just about every night. In 1930, it became a movie house and the name was changed to Bay Theatre. Today, the building is called the State Theatre, but I call it just plain haunted!

If you don't believe me, read on and discover the spooky things that happen once the audiences go home, and the spirits have the run of the place.

Brenda Baker, the former customer service director at the State Theatre, agreed to share some of her strange experiences there. Once, when Brenda was in the building alone and preparing for the evening's show, she walked through the empty theater and suddenly heard sounds coming from the lobby. To her, it sounded as if the lobby was full of people laughing and chatting while waiting for a show to begin.

Brenda was puzzled. Why had people arrived so early? And, more importantly, how had they all gotten into the lobby? She rushed down the aisle and threw open the lobby doors. What she found left her chilled right down to her bones.

The lobby was empty! She couldn't understand it. Moments before, she'd heard the sounds of a crowd of people. Now, there was not a single soul there. At least ... not a *living* soul. Brenda realized she had just encountered some of the theater's supernatural guests. And she definitely did not want to experience that again!

Brenda decided she would never walk through the empty lobby if she was alone in the theater again. If she was ever in the theater by herself, she always left through the back door. Sometimes, Brernda even ran out the building as fast as her legs would carry her, all to avoid coming face-to-face with the long-dead theatergoers who roam the building.

When Brenda shared her eerie encounter with other staff at the theater, she discovered she was not the only person who had experienced the paranormal in the building.

A coworker told Brenda about a shadowy figure lurking in the corners of the theater one morning. At first, the coworker thought it was just the shadow of another employee working in the theater that morning named Paul. Later, when the coworker went out to talk with Paul, she discovered she was in the theater alone. She had not seen Paul's shadow pass. Paul had not even been in the building. With a shiver, the coworker realized what she had seen was actually a ghost!

Paul also had his own strange experience to share. One day, he was alone in the theater working on the sound system when he

suddenly heard the basement door open. Paul paused and listened for a moment. He wasn't expecting anyone to join him in the theater that day. All at once, the basement door slammed shut and the lock on the door turned.

That certainly was strange. Could the wind have blown the door open—and maybe even closed? But when was the last time you saw the wind LOCK a door? That sounds a lot like the work of a ghost to me!

So, just who is this spirit in the theater? Many believe it is the ghost of Floyd Ackerman. In the 1940s, he managed the theater, where he was killed one night during an armed robbery.

Check Out Our Web Site
For All Our Exciting Events
www.statetheatrebaycity.com

State Theatre

Legend has it that Floyd, still wearing the tuxedo he wore to greet ticketholders all those years ago, appears throughout the theater. But it's not just employees who have seen the ghostly former manager!

Theater patron Carrie Smith tells a hair-raising story of her own encounter with Floyd.

In 2017, she was at the theater with her sister, Brittany. While taking a quick bathroom break during the show, Carrie entered one of the stalls and locked the door. That's when she noticed a pair of shiny, black men's shoes underneath the stall door. The toes of the shoes were pointed right at her!

Carrie cleared her throat to let whoever was inside those shoes know she was inside the stall.

The shoes did not move away from the door.

"Excuse me, someone is in here," Carrie

said. She hoped the person would back away, but instead, the shoes moved even closer to the stall door. Soon, the tips of the black shoes were just inches away from Carrie's toes!

Unsure of what else to do, Carrie pounded on the stall door with her fists. "Back up!" she yelled. "I am in here."

To her relief, the shoes took a step backward. But, before Carrie felt a sense of relief, she heard an eerie sound come from outside the stall: the sound of *fingernails* dragging against the stall door echoed in the bathroom. Then, through the crack in the door, Carrie saw a long finger glide across the edge of the door.

In a moment, her fear turned to rage. How

dare someone bother her while she was using the bathroom? She pulled the stall door open with all her might. She was ready to confront whoever was on the other side of the door.

Carrie's heart was racing when she walked out of the stall. She was ready to give the person in the black shoes a piece of her mind. She looked to the left and did not see anyone. She quickly swung her head to the right, but no one was there. Carrie was not going to let this person hide from her. She opened each stall door in the bathroom—but every stall was empty.

Carrie ran out into the hallway, determined to find the person who had bothered her. No one was there.

Still angry, Carrie returned to her seat in the theater.

"Someone was in the bathroom with me,

scratching on the stall door," Carrie whispered into her sister's ear.

Brittany told Carrie that it was probably just a kid playing a prank on her. Carrie disagreed.

"It was not a kid! I saw the shoes and pants. They definitely belonged to a grown man," insisted Carrie.

Brittany laughed off Carrie's concerns. But Carrie would have the last laugh after Brittany made her own trip to the restroom after the show.

Brittany waited in the line of theatergoers for her turn in the restroom. Carrie had refused to go with her and was waiting outside the theater.

When it was finally Brittany's turn, she thought about her sister as she entered the stall. She thought Carrie was the victim of a harmless prank, but she was glad there were other people in the restroom with her as she locked the stall door.

But, by the time Brittany finished using the toilet, she was the only person left in the restroom. Or, at least, that's what she thought.

She moved to the sink to wash her hands, but as she looked into the mirror, she noticed something move behind her reflection. When Brittany took a second glance, she saw someone standing behind her. It was a man wearing a tuxedo.

Startled, Brittany blurted out, "You do realize that this is the women's bathroom, right?"

As soon as the words left her mouth, the man behind her was gone. *Poof!* He disappeared into thin air!

Trembling in fear, Brittany raced out the bathroom and kept running until she met Carrie outside the theater. When she reunited with her sister, Brittany began to cry.

"I saw him! I saw the man. I believe you, and I'm sorry that I initially did not," Brittany croaked between sobs. As the pair rushed to their car, Brittany told Carrie everything that occurred in the theater restroom.

Once they were safely home, the sisters decided to do some research on the theater to understand what they had experienced that day. After reading about the history of the building, the girls believe that it was Floyd Ackerman's ghost they'd run into in the restroom.

"The State Theatre can now add the women's bathroom to their list of paranormal hotspots," Brittany said. "I totally thought he was alive, just like we are, until I literally saw him vanish. I am at a loss for words of what I have witnessed. This is truly one of the strangest things I have ever had happen in my life."

The sisters' story makes me wonder why Floyd Ackerman sticks around the old theater. Is his spirit trapped in the place where his life was taken? Does he reach out to the living in hopes that someone will help him cross over to the other side? Or, did he just love being in the theater so much in life . . . that he never wanted to leave?

I don't know the answer. But I *do* know I plan to steer clear of the restrooms in the State Theatre. I don't think I am brave enough to encounter the former theater manager, no matter the reason his spirit remains in the building. How about you? Are you brave enough for a trip to the State Theatre? If you do have the courage to visit, I hope you'll remember to use the bathroom BEFORE you arrive. There is just no telling who—or what!— you might encounter once you are all alone and locked inside the bathroom stall!

A Ghostly Goodbye

Thanks for exploring the spooky side of Bay City with us!

From the historic USS *Edson* to the spooky State Theatre, ghosts seem to be everywhere in Bay City. All this ghost talk might have sent you hiding under your covers, hoping to never encounter a ghost. Or, maybe it's inspired you to do your own paranormal investigations.

If you *do* decide to go exploring in hopes of having your own ghostly encounter, watch out! You just might get more than you bargained for! After all, ghosts that seem a little spooky in the book just might be terrifying in real life!

If you seek out the spirits for yourself, follow a few basic rules. Stick to places you are allowed to enter. Many people do not welcome ghost hunters on their property. If you get permission to seek out spirits, make sure your ghostly adventure is a safe one. Remember to stay in a group, take notes, and always—and I do mean ALWAYS!—watch your back.

You never know who, or what, might be right behind you!

Anna Lardinois tingles the spines of Milwaukee locals and visitors through her haunted, historical walking tours known as Gothic Milwaukee. The former English teacher is an ardent collector of stories, an avid walker, and a sweet treat enthusiast. She happily resides in a historic home in Milwaukee that, at this time, does not appear to be haunted. Visit her at www.annalardinois.com to find out more!

Check out some of the other *Spooky America* titles available now!

Spooky America was adapted from the creeptastic *Haunted America* series for adults. *Haunted America* explores historical haunts in cities and regions across America. Here's more from the original *Haunted Bay City, Michigan* author, Nicole Beauchamp:

Visit Nicole on Instagram: @authornicolebeauchamp